Clowns
IN CROSS STITCH

Julie Hasler

For Paul Human

THE CHARTS

Some of the designs in this book are very detailed and due to inevitable space limitations, the charts may be shown on a comparatively small scale; in such cases, readers may find it helpful to have the particular chart with which they are currently working enlarged.

THREADS

The projects in this book were all stitched with DMC stranded cotton embroidery threads. The keys given with each chart also list thread combinations for those who wish to use Anchor or Madeira threads. It should be pointed out that the shades produced by different companies vary slightly, and it is not always possible to find identical colours in a different range.

First published in 1996 by Merehurst Limited
Ferry House, 51-57 Lacy Road, Putney, London SW15 1PR
Text, photography & illustrations © Copyright 1996 Merehurst Limited
ISBN 1 85391 516 5

A catalogue record for this book is available from the British Library.

Edited by Diana Lodge
Designed by Maggie Aldred
Photography by Juliet Piddington
Illustrations by John Hutchinson
Typesetting by Dacorum Type & Print, Hemel Hempstead
Colour separation by Fotographics Limited, UK – Hong Kong
Printed in Hong Kong by Wing King Tong

Merehurst is the leading publisher of craft books and has an excellent range of titles to suit all levels. Please send to the address above for our free catalogue, stating the title of this book.

CONTENTS

Introduction   4

Basic Skills   4

Nightdress Case   8

Alphabet Picture   12

Clown Towels   16

Baby's Coverlet   20

Clown Faces   24

Smiling Cushions   28

Toy Bag   32

Photograph Frames   36

Acknowledgements   40

$\mathscr{I}$NTRODUCTION

The story of the clown goes back centuries because, by tradition, wherever people gather, there is inevitably someone to make them laugh. In every era, there has been a notable clown of some kind - someone who has been laughed at and loved and so has gained a place in history.

Today's clowns owe so much to the clowns of yesteryear, not only in their comic antics, but also in the clothes they wear, and the way they paint their faces. For example, the out-sized trousers and shoes and the undersized jacket date back to costumes worn by clowns during the reign of Queen Elizabeth I. The collection of cheery clowns featured in these designs have been used to decorate a range of items, mainly for children, that will make delightful gifts; they include a toy bag, a coverlet for a baby's cot or crib, an alphabet picture to make learning fun, plus towels, cushions and photograph frames. The projects are all fully described, but the designs, of course, can easily be adapted for a wide range of items of your choice.

$\mathscr{B}$ASIC SKILLS

■

BEFORE YOU BEGIN

PREPARING THE FABRIC
Even with an average amount of handling, many evenweave fabrics tend to fray at the edges, so it is a good idea to overcast the raw edges, using ordinary sewing thread, before you begin.

THE INSTRUCTIONS
Each project begins with a full list of the materials that you will require. Note that the measurements given for the embroidery fabric include a minimum of 4cm (1¹/₂in) all around to allow for stretching it in a frame and preparing the edges to prevent them from fraying.

Many of the projects in this book use Aida fabric, which is woven in blocks. Other projects use evenweave Bellana fabric. Stitches are taken over one Aida block or one thread intersection of Bellana fabric. Each square of the chart represents one block or thread intersection, and each symbol on the chart represents a single cross stitch, its colour indicated by the symbol used. Start the cross stitch embroidery at the centre of the design unless otherwise indicated, working all cross stitches so that the top stitches always lie in the same direction.

Colour keys for stranded embroidery cottons – DMC, Anchor or Madeira – are given with each chart. It is assumed that you will need to buy one skein of each colour mentioned in a particular key, even though you may use less, but where two or more skeins are needed, this information is included in the main list of requirements.

To work from the charts, particularly those where several symbols are used in close proximity, some readers may find it helpful to have the chart enlarged so that the squares and symbols can be seen more easily. Many photocopying services will do this for a minimum charge.

Before you begin to embroider, always mark the centre of the design with two lines of basting stitches, one vertical and one horizontal, running from edge to edge of the fabric, as indicated by the arrows on the charts.

As you stitch, use the centre lines given on the chart and the basting threads on your fabric as reference points for counting the squares and threads to position your design accurately.

WORKING IN A HOOP

A hoop is the most popular frame for use with small areas of embroidery. It consists of two rings, one fitted inside the other; the outer ring usually has an adjustable screw attachment so that it can be tightened to hold the stretched fabric in place. Hoops are available in several sizes, ranging from 10cm (4in) in diameter to quilting hoops with a diameter of 38cm (15in). Hoops with table stands or floor stands attached are also available.

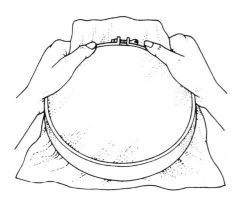

1 To stretch your fabric in a hoop, place the area to be embroidered over the inner ring and press the outer ring over it, with the tension screw released. Tissue paper can be placed between the outer ring and the embroidery, so that the hoop does not mark the fabric. Lay the tissue paper over the fabric when you set it in the hoop, then tear away the central embroidery area.

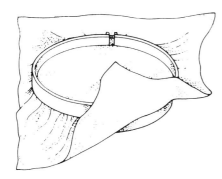

2 Smooth the fabric and, if necessary, straighten the grain before tightening the screw. The fabric should be evenly stretched.

WORKING IN A RECTANGULAR FRAME

Rectangular frames are more suitable for larger pieces of embroidery. They consist of two rollers, with tapes attached, and two flat side pieces, which slot into the rollers and are held in place by pegs or screw attachments. Available in different sizes, either alone or with adjustable table or floor stands, frames are measured by the length of the roller tape, and range in size from 30cm (12in) to 68cm (27in).

As alternatives to a slate frame, canvas stretchers and the backs of old picture frames can be used. Provided there is sufficient extra fabric around the finished size of the embroidery, the edges can be turned under and simply attached with drawing pins (thumb tacks) or staples.

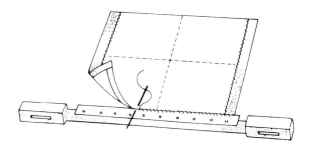

1 To stretch your fabric in a rectangular frame, cut out the fabric, allowing at least an extra 5cm (2in) all around the finished size of the embroidery. Baste a single 12mm (½in) turning on the top and bottom edges and oversew strong tape, 2.5cm (1in) wide, to the other two sides. Mark the centre line both ways with basting stitches. Working from the centre outward and using strong thread, oversew the top and bottom edges to the roller tapes. Fit the side pieces into the slots, and roll any extra fabric on one roller until the fabric is taut.

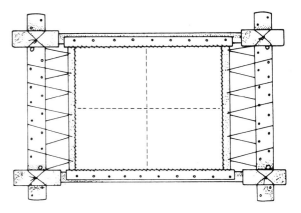

2 Insert the pegs or adjust the screw attachments to secure the frame. Thread a large-eyed needle (chenille needle) with strong thread or fine string and lace both edges, securing the ends around the intersections of the frame. Lace the webbing at 2.5cm (1in) intervals, stretching the fabric evenly.

EXTENDING EMBROIDERY FABRIC
It is easy to extend a piece of embroidery fabric, such as a bookmark, to stretch it in a hoop.

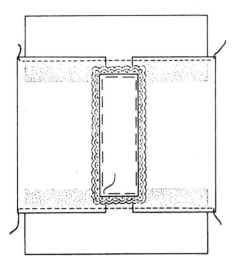

● Fabric oddments of a similar weight can be used. Simply cut four pieces to size (in other words, to the measurement that will fit both the embroidery fabric and your hoop) and baste them to each side of the embroidery fabric before stretching it in the hoop in the usual way.

THE STITCHES

BACKSTITCH
Backstitch is used in the projects to give emphasis to a particular foldline, an outline or a shadow. The

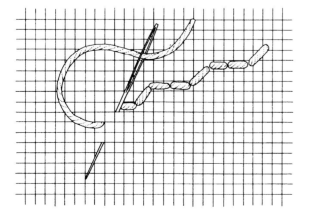

stitches are worked over the same number of threads as the cross stitch, forming continuous straight or diagonal lines.
● Make the first stitch from left to right; pass the needle behind the fabric and bring it out one stitch length ahead to the left. Repeat and continue in this way along the line.

CROSS STITCH
For all cross stitch embroidery, the following two methods of working are used. In each case, neat rows of vertical stitches are produced on the back of the fabric.

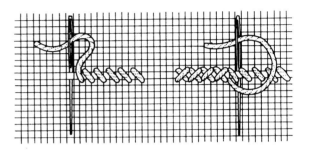

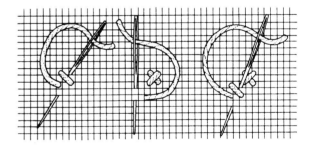

● When stitching large areas, work in horizontal rows. Working from right to left, complete the first row of evenly spaced diagonal stitches over the number of threads specified in the project instructions. Then, working from left to right, repeat the process. Continue in this way, making sure each stitch crosses in the same direction.
● When stitching diagonal lines, work downwards, completing each stitch before moving to the next.

WORKING WITH WASTE CANVAS
The waste canvas technique has been used for the designs in 'Clown Faces'. Waste canvas, quite simply, provides a removable grid over which you can stitch on unevenly-woven fabrics. Once the design has been stitched, the canvas is removed. Firstly, determine the size of the design, and cut a piece of canvas that allows a border of at least 5cm

(2in) all around. Baste the waste canvas to the design area of the fabric/item you are using. Stitch your design in the usual way, making sure it is centred on the fabric/item. When stitching is complete, remove the basting stitches and lightly dampen the canvas with water. Slowly and gently pull out the threads of canvas, *one at a time,* using a pair of tweezers. Don't hurry this process, as it could result in spoiling your stitching. You may need to re-dampen stubborn threads that will not pull out.

FINISHING

TO BIND AN EDGE

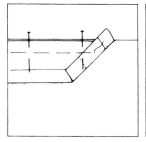 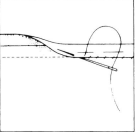

1 Open out the turning on one edge of the bias binding and pin in position on the right side of the fabric, matching the fold to the seamline. Fold over the cut end of the binding. Finish by overlapping the starting point by about 12mm (½in). Baste and machine stitch along the seamline.

2 Fold the binding over the raw edge to the wrong side, baste and, using matching sewing thread, neatly hem to finish.

LIGHTWEIGHT FABRICS

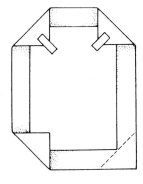 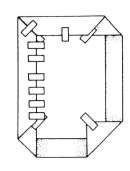

1 Place embroidery face down, with the cardboard centred on top, and basting and pencil lines

matching. Begin by folding over the fabric at each corner and securing it with masking tape.

2 Working first on one side and then the other, fold over the fabric on all sides and secure it firmly with pieces of masking tape, placed about 2.5cm (1in) apart. Also neaten the mitred corners with masking tape, pulling the fabric tightly to give a firm, smooth finish.

HEAVIER FABRICS

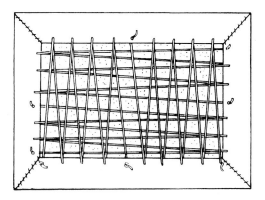

● Lay the embroidery face down, with the cardboard centred on top; fold over the edges of the fabric on opposite sides, making mitred folds at the corners, and lace across, using strong thread. Repeat on the other two sides. Finally, pull up the stitches fairly tightly to stretch the fabric firmly over the cardboard. Overstitch the mitred corners.

Nightdress Case

Make this colourful nightdress case to tuck away your child's nightie or pyjamas during the day. Lightly padded, trimmed with ribbon bows, and featuring an acrobatic clown doing the splits, it will brighten up any bedroom.

NIGHTDRESS CASE

YOU WILL NEED

For the nightdress case, measuring
45cm × 33cm (17³/₄in × 13in):

94cm × 47.5cm (37in × 18³/₄in) of sky blue,
14-count Aida fabric
Stranded embroidery cotton in the colours given
in the panel
No24 tapestry needle
Sewing thread to match the fabric
94cm × 47.5cm (37in × 18³/₄in) of lightweight
polyester batting
94cm × 47.5cm (37in × 18³/₄in) of lightweight
cotton fabric for the lining
1.12m (44in) of ribbon, 2.5cm (1in) wide,
in a contrast colour

●

THE EMBROIDERY

Prepare the edges of the fabric (see page 4); baste a line across the width, 7.5cm (3in) up from the bottom edge, to mark the baseline of the embroidery, and another 28.5cm (11¹/₂in) up from the bottom edge (this marks off the area for the front flap), then baste horizontal and vertical lines across the embroidery area.

Complete the cross stitching, working from the centre and using two strands of embroidery thread in the needle. Finish with the backstitching, using one strand of thread in the needle. Gently steam press the embroidery from the wrong side.

MAKING THE NIGHTDRESS CASE

Place the embroidered fabric face down on a flat surface; carefully smooth the batting on top; pin and baste the two together (12mm/¹/₂in seam allowance); trim the batting back almost to the basting line, and catch-stitch around the edge.

Make a single 12mm (¹/₂in) turning across the width (not flap edge) of the fabric and baste. With right sides facing, fold the pocket front section over for 32cm (12¹/₂in); baste, and machine stitch to form the pocket. Trim the corners and turn right side out.

Make a single turning on the short edge of the lining fabric and repeat as for the top fabric, but do not turn the pocket to the right side.

With right sides of the top fabric and lining together, baste and stitch around the flap, finishing

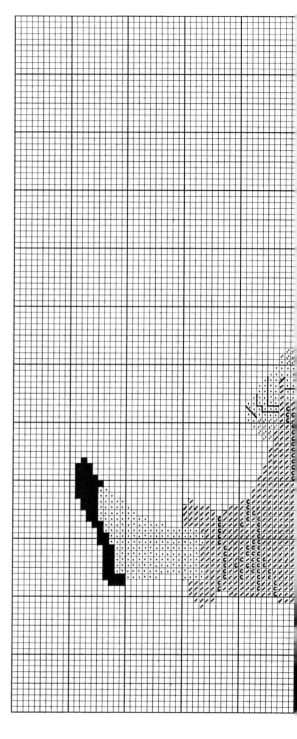

just above the side seams. Trim the corners and turn the flap through to the right side. Slip the lining into the pocket and slipstitch the top edges together, easing the turning so that the stitching is on the inside. Remove the basting stitches.

Cut the ribbon into two equal lengths; make two bows and catch-stitch them to the flap of the nightdress case diagonally across the corners, as shown in the photograph.

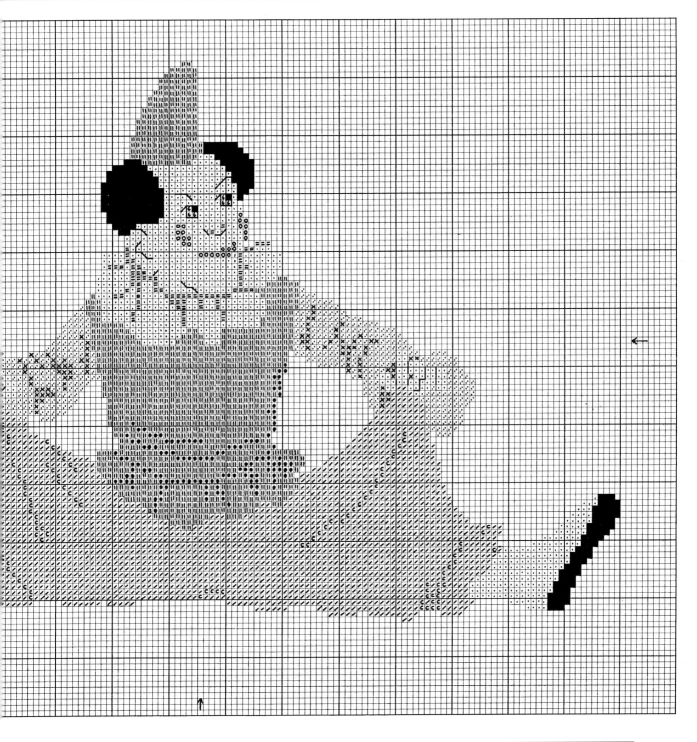

THE SPLITS ▲		DMC	ANCHOR	MADEIRA			DMC	ANCHOR	MADEIRA
C	Deep canary yellow	972	303	0107	‖	Dark violet	552	100	0713
=	Pale grey	415	398	1803	X	Medium garnet red	815	43	0513
●	Very dark violet	550	101	0714	○	Bright orange red	606	335	0209
·∴	Christmas red	321	47	0510		Light steel grey*	318	399	1808
6	Medium delft blue	799	130	0910					
╱	Dark lemon yellow	444	291	0108					
■	Black	310	403	Black					
·	White	White	2	White					

Note: backstitch, using light steel grey* (used for bks only) for hands and face, and black for eyes and eyebrows.

Alphabet Picture

Learning can be fun - teach your children their alphabet and numbers with the help of this colourful clown, juggling with letters. The bright colours make the picture an attractive addition to a nursery or a child's bedroom.

ALPHABET PICTURE

YOU WILL NEED

For the picture, measuring 48.5cm × 41cm
(19in × 16in) unframed:

*56.5cm × 49cm (22in × 19in) of white,
14-count Aida fabric
Stranded embroidery cotton in the colours given in
the panel
No24 tapestry needle
48.5cm × 41cm (19in × 16in) of mounting board
Picture frame of your choice*

Note The embroidery can either be set directly in a
frame or within a mount. A double mount was used
here, to create a two-tone border around the picture.

•

THE EMBROIDERY

Prepare the fabric, marking the horizontal and
vertical centre lines with basting stitches in a light-
coloured thread, and stretch it in a frame (see page
5). Following the chart, start the embroidery at the
centre of the design, using two strands of thread in
the needle. Finish with the backstitching, using one
strand of thread in the needle.

Leaving the basting stitches in position, gently
steam press the finished embroidery on the wrong
side.

MOUNTING

You can use either of the methods described on page
6 to mount your finished embroidery, using the bast-
ed centre lines as guidelines to ensure that you centre the embroidery over the mounting board. To
achieve a smooth finish, you may find that it is helpful to secure the fabric to one edge of the board with
pins, working from the centre point out to both corners, and then repeat for the opposite side, to make
sure that the fabric is even and taut. Secure with
tape or lacing, and then repeat for the remaining
sides. Carefully remove basting stitches from the
mounted embroidery.

If you are setting the mounted fabric in the frame
yourself, use rustproof pins to secure the backing
board, and seal the back of the picture with broad
tape, to ensure that dust cannot enter the frame.

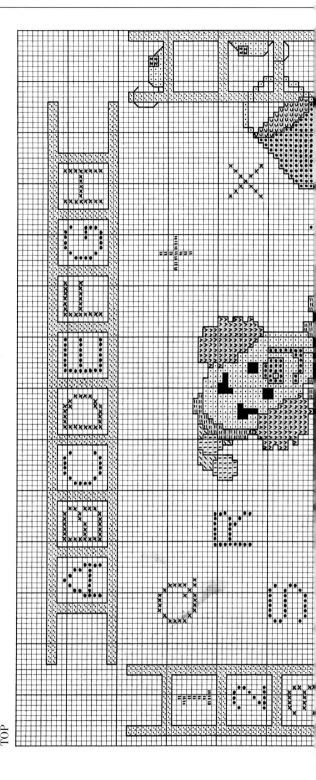

TOP

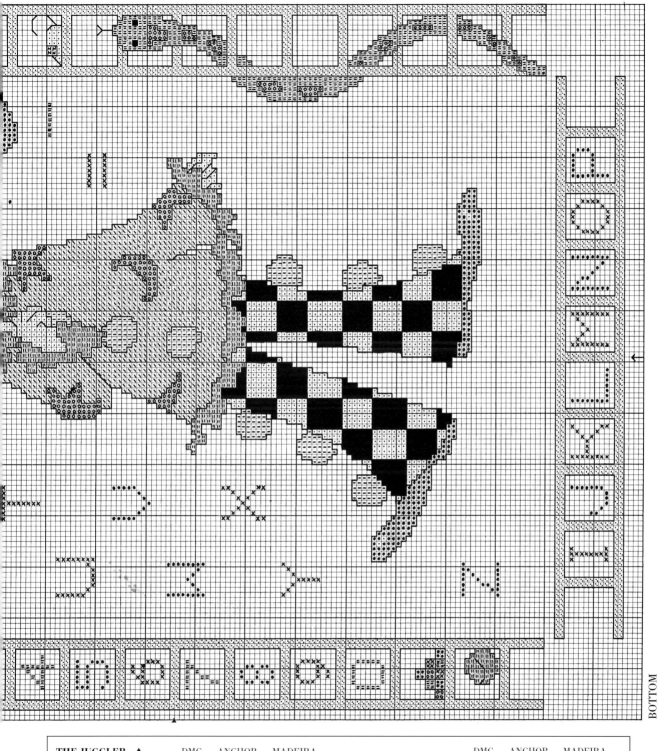

BOTTOM

THE JUGGLER ▲	DMC	ANCHOR	MADEIRA			DMC	ANCHOR	MADEIRA
● Bright Christmas red	666	46	0210	⊡ Tan brown		436	363	2011
X Royal blue	797	132	0912	⊡ White		White	2	White
‖ Dark emerald green	910	228	1301	Z Peach		353	8	0304
■ Black	310	403	Black	◿ Dark lilac		333	119	0903
= Medium cranberry	602	63	0702	V Pumpkin orange		971	316	0203
I Bright chartreuse green	704	256	1308	C Garnet red		816	20	0512
◯ Dark lemon yellow	444	291	0108	*Note: backstitch with black.*				

Clown Towels

Children of any age would be delighted to receive one of these 'tumbling clown' towels as a gift. The blues, purples, pinks and yellows used in the designs make them suitable for towels in a wide range of colours.

CLOWN TOWELS

For each embroidered towel:

*A strip of white, 14-count Aida band,
10cm (4in) deep and 2.5cm (1in) longer than the
width of your towel
Stranded embroidery cotton in the colours given in
the panel
No24 tapestry needle
White sewing thread
Towel of your choice*

Note You can, as here, stitch Aida band to any
suitable towel. Alternatively, you can purchase
towels that have an Aida band either inset into the
towel or already attached, along one long edge only
(for suppliers, see page 40).

THE EMBROIDERY

Mark the centre of the Aida band both ways with
lines of basting stitches. Before you begin to
stitch, work out how many repeats/clowns will fit
comfortably across the width of your chosen towel.
To achieve a balanced effect, calculate this by
working from the centre outwards, bearing in mind
that you must leave a 12mm (½in) seam allowance
at each short end. You can easily change the number of empty Aida blocks between clowns, if necessary. There is ample thread for several repeats of
these designs; for variety, you might choose to
change around the colours of the outfits on repeat-
ed motifs.

Starting from the centre and working outwards,
stitch the cross stitch design on the Aida band, using
two strands of thread in the needle and making sure
that the top stitches lie in the same direction
throughout. Finish with the backstitching, this time
using one strand of thread in the needle. Gently
steam press the embroidery from the wrong side and
remove basting stitches.

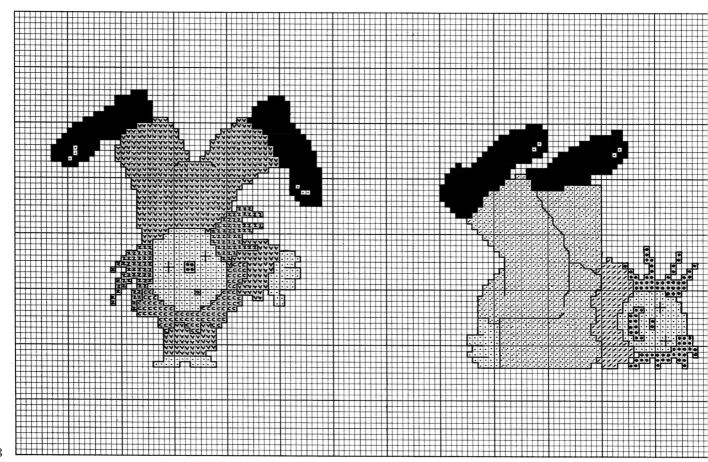

MAKING UP

Turn under a 12mm (½in) hem at each short end, and baste the Aida band to the towel in the desired position. When you are happy with the result, machine stitch the band to the towel.

TUMBLING CLOWNS		DMC	ANCHOR	MADEIRA
Z	Chartreuse green	703	238	1307
●	Bright Christmas red	666	46	0210
·	White	White	2	White
X	Aqua	959	186	1113
C	Periwinkle blue	340	118	0902
L	Cranberry	603	62	0701
⁄	Fuchsia purple	3608	86	0709
V	Medium yellow	744	301	0112
■	Royal blue	797	132	0912
II	Very light cranberry	605	50	0613
=	Nile green	954	204	1211
▼	Light pumpkin orange	970	316	0204
··	Delft blue	809	130	0909
	Medium steel grey*	317	400	1714

Note: backstitch with medium steel grey (used for bks only).*

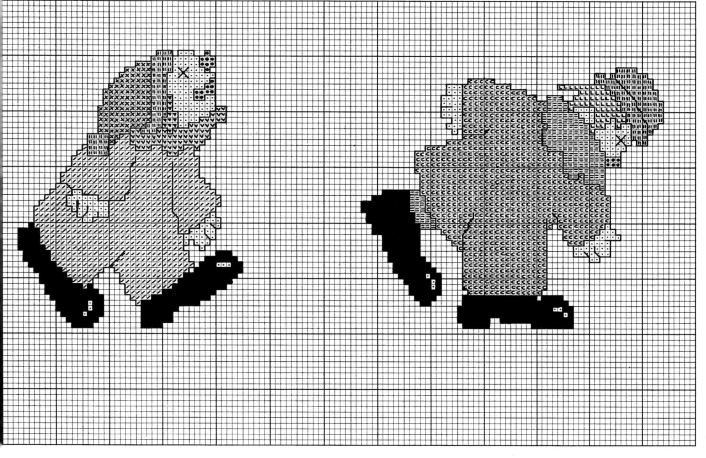

Baby's Coverlet

Could any child - or mother - resist these bright, jolly clowns? This wonderfully soft and practical Afghan fabric, featuring 13cm (5in) squares suitable for small cross stitch motifs, is easily washable, making it ideal for a baby's coverlet.

BABY'S COVERLET

YOU WILL NEED

For the coverlet, measuring 86cm × 104cm (34in × 41in):

92cm × 110cm (37in × 44in) of Anne Afghan fabric
Stranded embroidery cotton in the colours given in the panel
No26 tapestry needle
Matching sewing thread

●

THE EMBROIDERY

Following the diagram, cut the fabric to size. If you are securing the fringe by machine, stitch a zigzag border all around, as indicated. Mark the centre lines of each design with basting stitches, and mount the fabric in a hoop, following the instructions on page 5. Referring to the appropriate chart, complete each design, starting at the centre of each and using two strands in the needle for the cross stitching, and one for the backstitching.

COMPLETING THE COVERLET

Trim the fabric to the final size. To make the fringe, remove fabric threads one at a time until you reach the zigzag stitch line. Brush out the fringe with a stiff brush.

HEMSTITCH

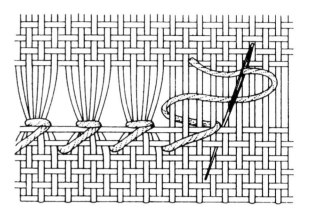

To finish with a traditional hem-stitched and fringed edge, remove a single thread from the fabric at the hem-line (the start of the fringe). Bring the needle out on the right side, two threads below the drawn-thread line. Working from left to right, pick up either two or three threads, as shown in the diagram. Bring the needle out again and insert it behind the fabric, to emerge two threads down, ready to make the next stitch. Before reinserting the needle, pull the thread tight, so that the bound threads form a neat group. To complete the fringe, remove the weft threads below the hemstitching.

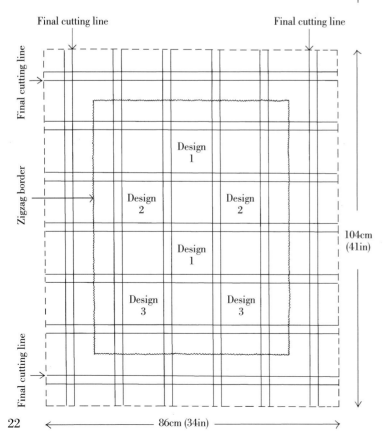

Final cutting line

Final cutting line

Final cutting line

Zigzag border

Final cutting line

Design 1

Design 2

Design 2

Design 1

Design 3

Design 3

104cm (41in)

86cm (34in)

MUSICAL CLOWNS ▶	DMC	ANCHOR	MADEIRA
· White	White	2	White
⁄ Dark lemon yellow	444	291	0108
C Light steel grey	318	399	1808
○ Tangerine orange	740	316	0202
■ Black	310	403	Black
● Bright Christmas red	666	46	0210
II Dark delft blue	798	131	0911
V Medium emerald green	911	205	1214

Note: backstitch with black.

Clown Faces

Even the plainest of children's clothes can be turned into something special with these clown faces and (optional) numerals. With the use of the waste canvas technique, these small designs can be added to clothes made from non-evenweave fabrics, and you can also make a card to accompany your gift.

CLOWN FACES

YOU WILL NEED

To embroider either of these decorations on your chosen item of children's clothing:

16cm × 14cm (6¹/₄in × 5¹/₂in) of Zweigart's waste canvas (for suppliers see page 40), with 14 double threads per 2.5cm (1in)
Stranded embroidery cotton in the colours given in the appropriate panel
No24 tapestry needle
Fine tweezers
Waterspray

For each matching card, measuring 20cm × 15cm (8in × 6in):

24cm × 19cm (9¹/₂in × 7¹/₂in) of white, 18-count Aida fabric
A piece of iron-on interfacing, approximately 15cm (6in) square (optional)
Stranded embroidery cotton in the colours given in

the appropriate panel
No26 tapestry needle
Double-sided adhesive tape
Card mount (for suppliers see page 40)

•

THE EMBROIDERY

To ensure that your finished embroidery lies straight on the garment, align the blue threads of the canvas horizontally or vertically, either with the weave of the fabric or with the seams of the garment. Pin and baste the canvas centrally over the design area and remove the pins (see page 6).

Treat each pair of canvas threads as a single thread, and stitch the design as you would on any other evenweave fabric. Start stitching at the top of the design and work downwards, using two strands for the cross stitch, and one for the backstitch. When you have finished, remove the waste canvas threads, following the instructions on page 6.

If you choose to sew your design onto fabric which is dry-cleanable only, the canvas threads can be softened by rubbing them together (taking care

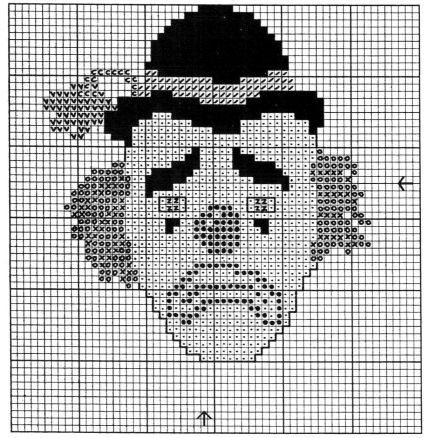

SAD CLOWN

not to damage the embroidery). It should then be possible to remove the threads one by one, without having to use water.

THE CARDS

Both cards are stitched in the same way and on the same type of fabric. Prepare the fabric, marking the centre lines of each design with basting stitches, and mount it in a small hoop, following the instructions on page 5. Referring to the appropriate chart, complete the cross stitching, using two strands in the needle, and finish with the backstitching, using one strand in the needle. Steam press on the wrong side if required.

It is not strictly necessary to use iron-on interfacing, but it helps to avoid wrinkles. If you are using interfacing, place it on the back of the embroidery; use a pencil to mark the basting/registration points on the interfacing and outer edge of the embroidery. Remove the basting stitches and iron the interfacing in place, aligning marks.

Trim the embroidery to measure about 12mm (^{1}/$_2$in) larger than the cut-out window, and then, making sure that the motif is placed in the middle by measuring an equal distance at each side of the marks, position the embroidery behind the window. Use double-sided tape to fix the embroidery into the card, then press the backing down firmly.

SMILING CLOWN

CLOWN FACES	DMC	ANCHOR	MADEIRA
■ Black	310	403	Black
╱ Very dark lavender	208	110	0804
◯ Medium tangerine orange	741	304	0201
✕ Medium burnt orange	946	332	0207
· White	White	2	White
● Bright Christmas red	666	46	0210
V Dark lemon yellow	444	291	0108
C Chartreuse green	703	238	1307
Z Medium delft blue	799	130	0910

Note: backstitch with black.

For a birthday card, you might like to stitch the appropriate number as given in the chart below.

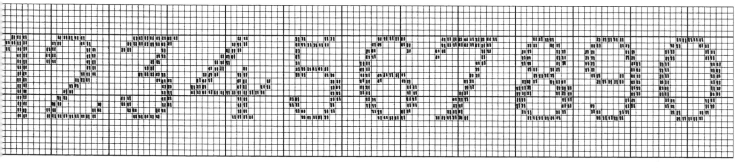

Smiling Cushions

These striking cushions, with their cheerful clown faces, are simple to make and will brighten up any room, either scattered on the bed or on a favourite chair. Use washable pads, so that you do not need to remove the covers for cleaning.

SMILING CUSHIONS

YOU WILL NEED

For each cushion, measuring 35.5cm (14in) square:

*43cm (17in) square of white, 14-count Aida fabric
38cm (15in) square of contrast fabric,
to back your cushion
Stranded embroidery cotton in the colours given in
the appropriate panel
No24 tapestry needle
35.5cm (14in) square cushion pad
Sewing thread to match both the cushion and the
bias binding
1.6m (1²/₃yds) of bias binding 2.5cm (1in) wide, in a
contrasting colour*

•

THE EMBROIDERY

Prepare the fabric, marking the centre lines of the
design with basting stitches, and mount it in a hoop
or frame, following the instructions on page 5.
Referring to the appropriate chart, complete the
cross stitching, starting at the centre and using two
strands in the needle. Finish with the backstitching,
this time using a single strand in the needle. Steam
press on the wrong side.

MAKING UP THE CUSHION

Keeping the design centred, trim the embroidered
Aida fabric to measure the same size as the backing
fabric, and place them together, with wrong sides
facing. Pin and baste on three sides. Remove pins
and machine stitch around these three sides, 12mm
(¹/₂in) in from the raw edges of the fabric.

Remove basting stitches and insert the cushion
pad. Machine stitch the remaining edge closed in
the same manner. Trim all around the edges with the
bias binding (see page 6).

BALDING CLOWN	DMC	ANCHOR	MADEIRA			DMC	ANCHOR	MADEIRA
⧄ Royal blue	797	132	0912	Z Delft blue		809	130	0909
● Medium burnt orange	946	332	0207	· White		White	2	White
‖ Pumpkin orange	971	316	0203	T Medium garnet red		815	43	0513
V Medium emerald green	911	205	1214	O Bright Christmas red		666	46	0210
■ Black	310	403	Black	L Pale grey		415	398	1803
C Blue grey	927	849	1708	6 Medium blue grey		926	779	1707
— Lemon yellow	307	289	0104					
X Medium cranberry	602	63	0702					

*Note: backstitch with black around the eyes, pale grey for the teeth,
and bright Christmas red for the top lip.*

TOP

BALDING CLOWN

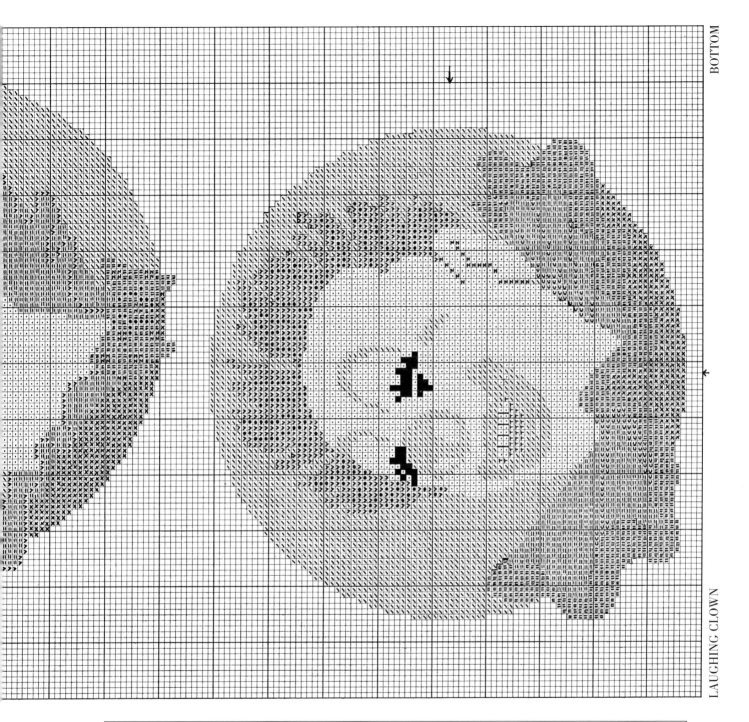

LAUGHING CLOWN	DMC	ANCHOR	MADEIRA			DMC	ANCHOR	MADEIRA
X Medium cranberry	602	63	0702	C Deep canary yellow		972	303	0107
II Pumpkin orange	971	316	0203	T Medium garnet red		815	43	0513
● Medium emerald green	911	205	1214	= Lemon yellow		307	289	0104
∕ Bright Christmas red	666	46	0210	· White		White	2	White
6 Medium burnt orange	946	332	0207	■ Black		310	403	Black
V Bright chartreuse green	704	256	1308					
Z Pale grey	415	398	1803	*Note: backstitch the teeth with pale grey.*				

Toy Bag

Suitable for a child of any age, this toy bag will make an extremely practical gift, and a bright and attractive feature in the playroom or nursery. The bag has a simple drawstring top and is both large and strong enough to hold many small toys. Alternatively, it could prove equally useful as a laundry bag.

TOY BAG

YOU WILL NEED

For a toy bag, measuring 48cm × 35.5cm (19in × 14in):

50.5cm × 38cm (20in × 15in) of white pearl, 11-count Aida fabric
Stranded embroidery cotton in the colours given in the panel
Matching sewing thread
No24 tapestry needle
Three pieces of white cotton fabric, each measuring 50.5cm × 38cm (20in × 15in), for the backing and lining
2.5m (2½yds) of white cord, 6mm (¼in) in diameter

•

THE EMBROIDERY

Prepare the Aida fabric, marking the centre lines of the design with basting stitches; ensure that there is a clearance around the design area of 9cm (3½in) at the sides, and 6.5cm (2½in) at the bottom. Mount it in a hoop or frame, following the instructions on page 5. Referring to the chart, complete the cross stitching, using three strands in the needle. Embroider the main area first, then finish with the backstitching, using two strands of thread in the needle. Steam press on the wrong side.

MAKING THE BAG

Place the Aida and one piece of the white cotton fabric right sides together. Taking a 12mm (½in) seam allowance, stitch the side seams down from the top for 4cm (1½in). Leave a gap of 2.5cm (1in), then recommence stitching the side seams to the bottom, as shown in diagram A.

Press the side seams open around the gap and top stitch 6mm (¼in) from the edge, as shown in diagram B. Stitch the bottom seam. Turn to the right side and press, trying not to iron over the embroidery.

Place the two remaining pieces of cotton fabric right sides together, and stitch the side seams. Stitch the bottom seam, leaving an opening of 10cm (4in) for turning inside out (see diagram C). *Do not turn yet.*

Place the outer bag into the lining, with right sides together, and stitch around the top edge. Turn right side out, easing through the opening at the bottom of the lining. Hand-stitch the lining together at the bottom.

Press the top edge of the bag along the seam. Topstitch around the bag 6mm (¼in) above the cord opening and again 6mm (¼in) below, as shown in diagram D. Thread the cord twice through the casement made by the two rows of stitches, and tie the ends together.

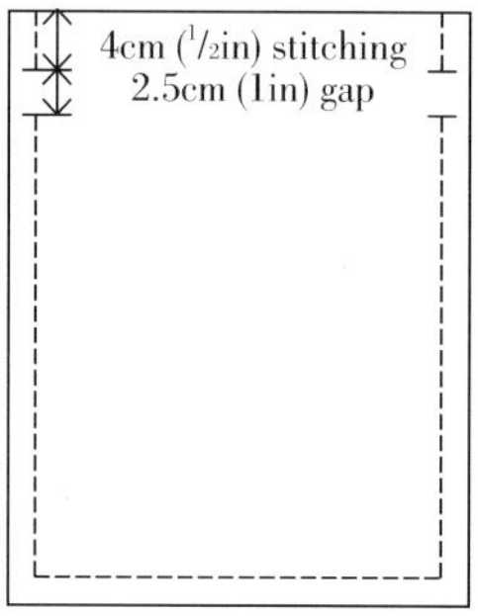

A

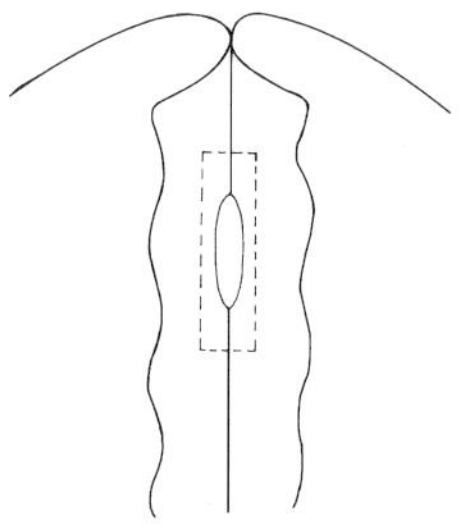

B

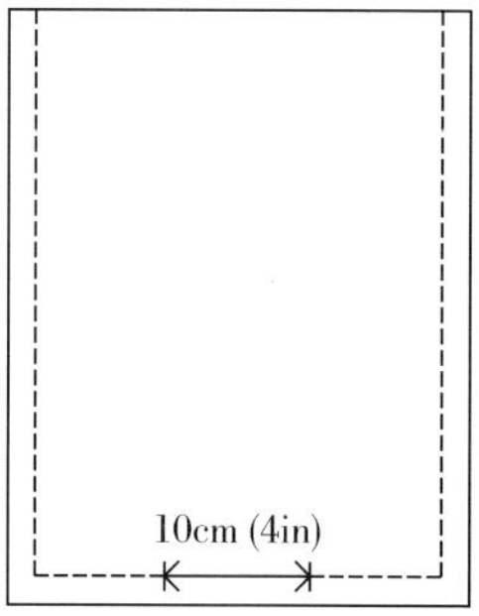

C

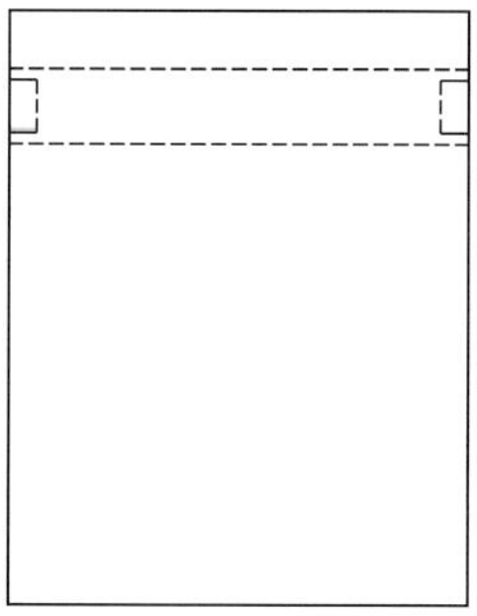

D

TOY CLOWN ▶		DMC	ANCHOR	MADEIRA
II	Light cranberry	604	305	0504
/	Light emerald green	912	209	1212
■	Black	310	403	Black
⁛	Off white	746	386	0101
X	Lemon yellow	307	289	0104
·	White	White	2	White
●	Bright Christmas red	666	46	0210
○	Bright orange	608	333	0206
=	Tan brown	436	363	2011
V	Pale grey	415	398	1803

Note: backstitch with black.

Photograph Frames

These enchanting photograph frames will make a cheerful and amusing addition to your home, whether displayed individually or as a pair. Either of the two designs would make a lovely present for an adult or a child.

PHOTOGRAPH FRAMES

YOU WILL NEED

For each Pierrot frame measuring 30.5cm × 23cm
(12in × 9in):

*38cm × 30.5cm (15in × 12in) of 20-count,
silver fleck Bellana fabric
Stranded embroidery cotton in the colours given in
the appropriate panel
No26 tapestry needle
30.5cm × 23cm (12in × 9in) of white
mounting board
Scalpel, craft knife or scissors
Masking tape
Craft adhesive
9cm (3¹/₂in) of white ribbon, 6mm (¹/₄in) wide,
for a hanging loop
Thin white card to back the frame*

THE EMBROIDERY

For each frame, prepare the fabric and stretch it in a hoop or frame (see page 5). Embroider the design in the relevant bottom corner of the fabric, 6.5cm (2¹/₂in) in from the raw edges of the fabric at the side and bottom. Using one strand of thread in the needle

PIERROT WITH A FLOWER ▼		DMC	ANCHOR	MADEIRA
■	Black	310	403	Black
·	White	White	2	White
∕	Pale grey	415	398	1803
Z	Medium shell grey	452	906	1807
●	Light red	350	11	0213
∴	Light lavender	211	342	0801
V	Dark lavender	209	105	0803
X	Very dark lavender	208	110	0804
‖	Medium steel grey	317	400	1714
⌐	Light shell grey	453	375	1806
	Rich red*	817	9046	0211

Note: backstitch the eyebrows and eyelid with black; use medium shell grey for the face, and rich red* (used for bks only) for the lips.

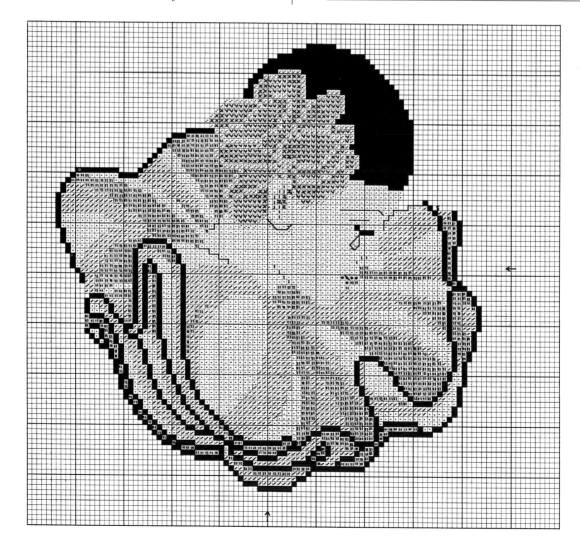

throughout, complete the cross stitching first, and finish off with the backstitching. Leaving the basting stitches in at this stage, as guidelines, gently press the finished embroidery on the wrong side with a steam iron.

MAKING THE FRAME

Carefully cut out a window from the mounting board: the windows of the frames shown here measure 9.5cm (3³⁄₄in) square, and are positioned 5cm (2in) in from the top and side edges of the mounting board, diagonally opposite the embroidery. You can, however, cut the window to whatever size or shape you wish.

Place your embroidery face down on a firm, flat surface and, using the basting stitches as a guide, position the mounting board on top of it. Next, mark the cut-out on the fabric with a soft pencil. Remove the basting stitches and, using a sharp pair of scissors, make a small nick in the centre of the marked cut-out in the fabric, and cut diagonally from the centre up to each marked corner. Place the mounting board over the fabric again, and fold the

triangles of fabric to the back of the board, securing them with masking tape. Next, fold in the outer edges of fabric, mitring the corners and securing them with tape (see page 7).

Using tape or craft adhesive, secure your chosen photograph in position. Form the ribbon into a loop, and secure it to the back of the frame with adhesive. To neaten the back of the frame, cut a piece of white card to the same size as the frame and secure it to the frame with adhesive.

PIERROT ▼		DMC	ANCHOR	MADEIRA
■	Black	310	403	Black
·	White	White	2	White
II	Medium steel grey	317	400	1714
●	Light red	350	11	0213
Z	Medium shell grey	452	906	1807
I	Light shell grey	453	375	1806
∕	Pale grey	415	398	1803
	Rich red*	817	9046	0211

Note: backstitch the eyebrows with black; use medium shell grey for face, and rich red* (used for bks only) for the lips.

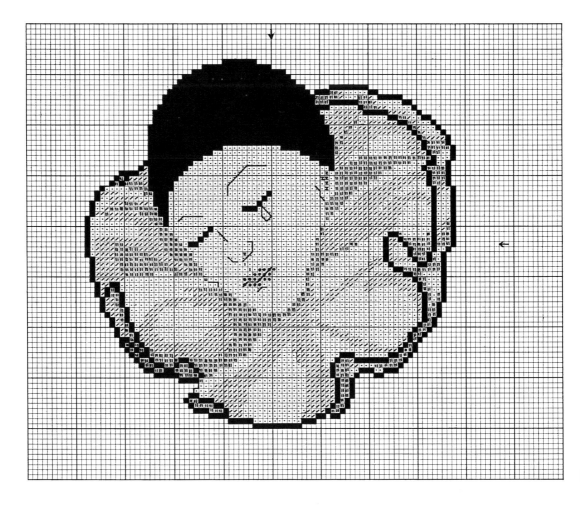

ACKNOWLEDGEMENTS

The author would like to thank the following people for their help with this book.

For the embroidery work Andrea Martin, Judy Riggins, Lesley Buckerfield, Odette Coe, Angela Eardley, Lynda Potter and Diana Hewitt.

For making up the projects Connie Woolcott.

Thanks are also due to DMC Creative World Ltd, for supplying fabrics, threads and card mounts.

Suppliers request that a stamped self-addressed envelope be enclosed with all enquiries.

SUPPLIERS

The following mail order company has supplied some of the basic items needed for making up the projects in this book:

Framecraft Miniatures Limited
372/376 Summer Lane
Hockley
Birmingham, B19 3QA
England
Telephone: 0121 212 4442

Addresses for Framecraft stockists worldwide
Ireland Needlecraft Pty Ltd
2-4 Keppel Drive
Hallam,
Victoria 3803
Australia

Danish Art Needlework
PO Box 442, Lethbridge
Alberta T1J 3Z1
Canada

Sanyei Imports
PO Box 5, Hashima Shi
Gifu 501-62
Japan

The Embroidery Shop
286 Queen Street
Masterton
New Zealand

Anne Brinkley Designs Inc.
246 Walnut Street
Newton
Mass. 02160
USA

S A Threads and Cottons Ltd.
43 Somerset Road
Cape Town
South Africa

For information on your nearest stockist of embroidery cotton, contact the following:

DMC
(also distributors of Zweigart fabrics)

UK
DMC Creative World Limited
62 Pullman Road, Wigston
Leicester, LE8 2DY
Telephone: 0116 2811040

USA
The DMC Corporation
Port Kearney Bld.
10 South Kearney
N.J. 07032-0650
Telephone: 201 589 0606

AUSTRALIA
DMC Needlecraft Pty
P.O. Box 317
Earlswood 2206
NSW 2204
Telephone: 02599 3088

COATS AND ANCHOR

UK
Coats Paton Crafts
McMullen Road
Darlington
Co. Durham DL1 1YQ
Telephone: 01325 381010

USA
Coats & Clark
P.O. Box 27067
Dept CO1
Greenville SC 29616
Telephone: 803 234 0103

AUSTRALIA
Coats Paton Crafts
Thistle Street
Launceston
Tasmania 7250
Telephone: 00344 4222

MADEIRA

UK
Madeira Threads (UK) Limited
Thirsk Industrial Park
York Road, Thirsk
N. Yorkshire, YO7 3BX
Telephone: 01845 524880

USA
Madeira Marketing Limited
600 East 9th Street
Michigan City
IN 46360
Telephone: 219 873 1000

AUSTRALIA
Penguin Threads Pty Limited
25-27 Izett Street
Prahran
Victoria 3181
Telephone: 03529 4400